Motor skills

Motor development for individuals with Down syndrome – An overview

Ben Sacks and Sue Buckley

Summary – The term motor development covers a wide range of important human skills, from sitting, walking and running, to independent drinking, eating and dressing, to writing, drawing and using a keyboard, to sports and dance, and to work related skills such as operating machinery or packing. Most of us take our motor skills for granted, as most are performed easily and effectively without the need for conscious control, but, in fact, all movements require fast and complex control by the central nervous system, and motor control is still not fully understood by researchers in this field. In this overview, research into the development and control of movements in typically developing individuals is discussed, and compared with the research into the motor development of individuals with Down syndrome, in order to identify evidence-based principles on which to base effective interventions. The research studies indicate that the pattern of motor skill development for individuals with Down syndrome is largely one of delay rather than difference, though attention needs to be given to developing strength and balance, and that they learn most effectively visually, from imitating a model, rather than from verbal instruction. The most effective way in which to improve motor skills for any individual is with practice, and studies have shown that individuals with Down syndrome need more practice than typically developing individuals to improve their performance. Most teenagers and adults can continue to develop their motor skills and many will achieve high levels of skill if given the opportunity.

Series Editors

Sue Buckley and Gillian Bird

DSii-12-01-(en-gb) (April, 2003)

http://www.down-syndrome.info/library/dsii/12/01/

First published: April, 2003

ISBN: 1-903806-17-8

A publication of The Down Syndrome Educational Trust

The Sarah Duffen Centre, Belmont Street, Southsea,
Hampshire, PO5 1NA, United Kingdom.

Telephone	+44 (0)23 9285 5330
Facsimile	+44 (0)23 9285 5320
E-mail	enquiries@downsed.org
Web Site	http://www.downsed.org/

The Down Syndrome Educational Trust is a charity, registered in England and Wales (number 1062823).

Proceeds from this publication support future research, services and publications. The production of this book provides employment for adults with Down syndrome.

The rights of Ben Sacks and Sue Buckley to be identified as authors of this Work has been asserted by them in accordance with sections 77 and 78 of the Copyright, Designs and Patents Act 1988.

Note: Figure 3, p.18, from The development of Down's syndrome children (p.339) by Rauh, H., Rudinger, G., Bowman, T.G., Berry, P., Gunn, P.V. & Hayes, A. In M. Lamb & H. Keller (Eds.) *Infant development: Perspectives from German speaking countries,* 1991, Hillsdale, NJ: Lawrence Erlbaum Associates, Copyright 1991 by M. Lamb & H. Keller. Adapted with permission.

Concept and design: Frank Buckley and Linda Hall.

Typeset, printed and distributed by a wholly-owned subsidiary of The Down Syndrome Educational Trust:

DownsEd Limited
The Sarah Duffen Centre, Belmont Street,
Southsea, Hampshire, PO5 1NA.
United Kingdom.

Contents

Authors

Ben Sacks

Consultant Developmental Psychiatrist and Medical Adviser to The Down Syndrome Educational Trust, UK.
Formerly Professor of Developmental Psychiatry, Charing Cross and Westminster Medical Schools,
The University of London, London, UK.

Sue Buckley

Emeritus Professor of Developmental Disability, Psychology Department, University of Portsmouth, UK.
Director of Research and Training, The Down Syndrome Educational Trust, UK.

Acknowledgements

The authors would like to thank all of the children, families and colleagues that they have had the privilege to work with and learn from over many years.

The authors would also like to thank Mark Latash and Dale Ulrich, both experts on motor research in this field, for reading and commenting on an earlier draft of this book. However, the responsibility for the final content, and any errors, is solely that of the authors.

The authors and publisher would like to thank all the families who have provided the photographs used in this publication.

Terminology

The term 'learning difficulty' is used throughout this module as it is the term currently in common use in the United Kingdom. The terms 'mental retardation', 'intellectual impairment', and 'developmental disability' are equivalent terms, used in other parts of the world.

DOWN SYNDROME
issues and
information

Motor development for individuals with Down syndrome – An overview

Introduction

In the first year of life, infants begin to gain control over movements – they begin to be able to hold their heads steady, to reach out and grasp objects, to roll, sit and crawl and to hold cups or bottles for feeding. They then go on to walk, run, climb stairs, use a spoon, knife and fork, and dress themselves. Later they draw, write, use the computer, play football and dance. We tend to take our movement abilities for granted as, for most of us, they have developed effortlessly and most are carried out as we go through our day without conscious attention to them at all. However, there is a large research literature devoted to trying to understand how the brain controls our everyday movements so skilfully, and the processes are still not fully understood. In the first section of this overview we will discuss the current views of the motor research experts, as it is relevant to our understanding of progress for children with Down syndrome.

Many babies and young children with Down syndrome are late to reach the early motor milestones such as grasping, rolling, sitting, standing and walking. There is wide variability in progress, with some reaching these milestones as early as typically developing infants and some being particularly slow in achieving them. Most parents are advised that physiotherapy will help, but do we actually know the reasons for this slower progress in order to provide guidelines for effective therapy? Do we know if physiotherapy actually makes any difference to progress and, if so, how? Is the motor progress of children with Down syndrome just delayed (i.e. slower but otherwise the same as in other children) or is it actually different – due to physical differences in their muscles, ligaments or central nervous systems?

Whatever the answers to these questions, we know from our own practical experience and research that the majority of children with Down syndrome achieve all the basic motor skills necessary for everyday living and personal independence. They may be later to achieve them and their movements may seem a little clumsy or less refined as they carry out tasks but they still have adequate skill for daily competence. Many continue to improve and refine their abilities in daily tasks such as handwriting, making a cup of tea, and tying shoelaces, well into adult life. They may have more difficulty in becoming skilled in games and recreational activities but many individuals do reach high levels of achievement when given the opportunity.

Research into the motor development and motor skills of children and adults with Down syndrome is limited and, as we have studied the available information, we have come to believe that some unhelpful myths keep being repeated, without supporting evidence. One of these myths is hypotonia, or 'poor muscle tone'. Almost every article we have read has used hypotonia as an explanation, when in fact it probably plays little part in determining children's motor progress. We will return to this issue later.

In this overview, we consider four questions.

1. What do we know about motor development in typically developing children and the factors that may influence rates of progress or levels of skills achieved for different motor activities?

2. What do we know about the pattern of motor development usually seen in infants, children and teenagers with Down syndrome?

3. What do we know about the effects of therapeutic interventions?

4. Can we draw on these three sources of evidence to identify some principles for effective intervention and activity programmes for individuals with Down syndrome across the age range?

Before we can discuss motor skills, we need to recognise that the term covers a wide range of activities and actions, and we have divided them into somewhat arbitrary groups in order to more conveniently discuss therapies and interventions later.

What are motor skills?

The ability to move is essential to human development, and children develop a remarkable range of motor skills from the first year of life through to adult life. Some are essential to basic human development and others are specialised and optional. For practical purposes, motor skills can be considered under two main headings:

- basic skills necessary for everyday life activities, and

- recreational, employment or specialist skills which are optional and based on interests and aptitudes.

Basic skills include sitting, walking, running, climbing stairs, picking up objects, using cups, knives and forks, pouring drinks, dressing and managing fastenings, holding and using pencils, pens, scissors and using keyboards.

Recreational skills include skipping, throwing, catching, hitting and kicking balls, riding a tricycle or a bicycle, swimming, skiing and all sporting activities, playing a musical instrument and playing computer games. Employment skills may be specific to a particular job and involve learning to operate machinery. They may also be an extension of basic daily living skills, such as those used in catering or gardening work.

http://www.down-syndrome.info/library/dsii/12/01/

**DOWN SYNDROME
issues and
information**

See also:

- *Speech and language development for individuals with Down syndrome - An overview* [DSii-03-01]
- *Speech and language development for infants with Down syndrome (0-5 years)* [DSii-03-02]
- *Speech and language development for children with Down syndrome (5-11 years)* [DSii-03-04]
- *Speech and language development for teenagers with Down syndrome (11-16 years)* [DSii-03-06]

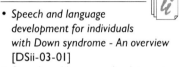

Basic skills are usually further divided into gross motor skills and fine motor skills.

- Gross motor skills are those concerned with whole body movement including sitting, walking, running and climbing stairs.

- Fine motor skills tend to be those requiring fine manipulation of fingers and hands including picking up objects, using cups, knives and forks, pouring drinks, dressing and managing fastenings, holding and using pencils, pens, scissors and keyboards.

These divisions are somewhat arbitrary and do not imply the use of separate parts of the motor system, as elements of gross motor control such as maintenance of balance and body posture play a part in carrying out all fine motor activities. However, they provide a useful practical way of dividing the whole range of possible motor skills and they link with the sources of therapy and teaching available to children and parents. Physiotherapists tend to be expert in the development of basic gross motor skills and occupational therapists tend to be experts in basic fine motor skills, although their skills will often overlap. Recreational skills tend to be taught by teachers, physical education experts, sports coaches and specialists such as music teachers. Employment skills may be taught by supervisors or job coaches.

We have not included speech-motor skills in this discussion, as the ability to talk, while a motor skill, is ill-understood, and is influenced by the ability to hear and store the sound patterns of words (phonology). Speech is therefore specialised and different, in at least some ways, from other motor skills. Some information on speech-motor development can be found in the speech and language books in this series.

Movement influences social and cognitive progress

While progress in basic gross and fine motor skills is important because the ability to carry out the movements has direct and practical benefit on a child's daily living and independence, motor progress is also important because these abilities influence social and cognitive development as well. The following list gives just a few examples of these links:

- being able to reach and grasp allows a child to begin to explore the characteristics of objects in his or her physical world;

- being able to sit increases the ability to use arms and hands for playing;

- being able to walk allows a child to carry toys and objects and to explore the world more effectively than crawling on hands and knees;

- being able to move independently also increases opportunities for social interaction and language learning. For example, once a child can move, they can go to see what happens when a visitor comes to the door or the telephone rings. They can follow their carers around so that they are talked to and included in everyday activities;

- being able to run, jump, climb and catch a ball increases a child's ability to join in games in the playground;

- being able to dance, swim or play football increases opportunities for leisure activities and friends, from childhood to adult life.

http://www.down-syndrome.info/library/dsii/12/01/
© Copyright 2003, The Down Syndrome Educational Trust. All Rights Reserved.
This page may not be reproduced without prior permission.

DSii-12-01-(en-gb)

I. What do we know about the development of motor skills in typically developing children?

In this section we consider first what we know about how all human movements are controlled and improved, and then what we know about the developmental progress of motor skills in children. We have provided some detail for the reader because a number of the explanations given for the motor delays of children with Down syndrome can only be discussed if one has some knowledge of the mechanisms involved in movement.

Movement control is complex

The mechanisms of motor control are complex and not yet fully understood.[1-5] The way in which ordinary movements, such as reaching for a cup or walking, are carried out is clearly immensely complicated. Each time the movement of picking up a cup is performed it is a unique movement pattern, as the distance to be reached, the angle at which the arm extends relative to the body, the size of the cup and the level of liquid in it, will vary. Similarly, when walking, each episode of walking is different as it may be over a different distance, at a different speed, on smooth or rough ground, uphill or against a wind. Research in the field of motor control is very active and during the last few decades increasingly sophisticated mathematical models have been developed to try and explain the way in which the brain carries out everyday movements.[1,3,4] The models are tested against actual data on how movements are performed.

All recent theories agree that some actions may be represented in the brain as partly prepared 'plans of action' or 'neuromotor programmes', but that as each action is carried out it is also controlled 'on-line' to ensure effectiveness in that particular situation. The learned neuromotor programmes provide 'feedforward' plans that are activated to initiate a movement and information from the senses and body provide continuous 'feedback' information. Both 'feedback' and 'feedforward' systems are used by the brain to carry out each effective movement. Every movement is unique in some of its features, even repeated actions such as reaching to pick up and put down the same cup in the same place several times. In the next section we consider some of the mechanisms involved in 'on-line' control and in learning neuromotor programmes.

Systems involved in movement control

Any movement requires the integrated action of the brain, nerves and muscles. As a movement is carried out, there is fast continuous control and adjustment occurring as the brain produces a coordinated action. Feedback of different kinds from the muscles and limbs, from vision and from balance systems is an integral part of all movement control as it is taking place. Figure 1 illustrates some of the relevant anatomy.

The central nervous system

It is known that all 'voluntary' movement is controlled by impulses from nerves that originate in the central nervous system, which consists of the brain and the spinal cord. With the exception of some basic reflexes (spinal reflexes), which may be mediated through the spinal cord, all coordinated movement sequences are determined by the brain. Although there are parts of the brain that are mainly concerned with the control of movement, such as

---

Movement control

Movement control is complex and not fully understood but two main features can be identified for practical purposes:

1. All movements require fast continuous control by the brain as they are carried out.

2. Over time, learned neuromotor programmes for movements are also used by the brain in the control of a movement.

The brain uses information from the vestibular system, from vision and from proprioception as movements proceed.

The brain provides instructions to the muscles, in order to carry out specific movements.

These instructions will take account of lax ligaments or less 'tone' in muscles to produce the desired movement.

The information processing capacities of an individual may influence movement.

DOWN SYNDROME issues and information

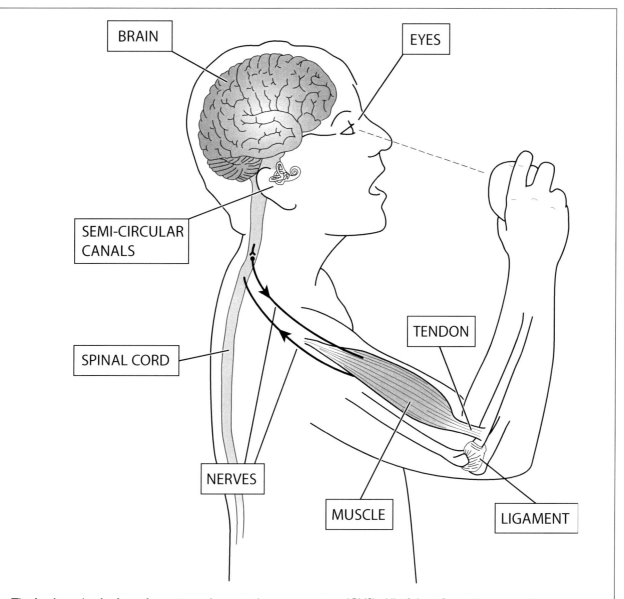

The **brain** and **spinal cord** constitute the central nervous system (CNS). All of the information processing necessary for producing coordinated movement takes place in the CNS.

The eyes obtain **visual** information about the environment and the body itself. This information is integrated with other types of information as part of the feedback system for muscular coordination.

The **semi-circular canals** near the inner ear (vestibular apparatus) provide information about the position of the head relative to horizontal and vertical planes (indicating upright, leaning or falling body positions) and acceleration (changes in speed). They are therefore important in maintaining balance.

The **peripheral nervous system** is that part of the nervous system which is concerned with motor control and it consists of motor (efferent) and sensory (afferent) nerves. Motor nerves carry information *from* the CNS, and control muscle contraction and relaxation. Sensory nerves carry feedback information from muscles, tendons and other tissues *to* the CNS.

Muscle is a tissue which, using the glucose and oxygen provided by the circulating blood, converts chemical energy into mechanical energy by contracting. Muscle contraction produces the movements involved in all body activities. Skeletal muscle moves the limbs, trunk and other parts of the body which are involved in so-called 'voluntary' movement. It is controlled by nerves from the CNS.

Tendons are cable-like structures which connect muscles to the muscle attachments on bones.

Ligaments are similar to tendons but generally attach bones to each other.

Figure 1. The coordination of motor control

http://www.down-syndrome.info/library/dsii/12/01/
DSii-12-01-(en-gb)

the cerebellum and the motor and pre-motor areas of the cortex, it is important to note that motor control is widely distributed in the brain, with many other areas being involved.

The muscles

The skeletal muscles are those which move the limbs, trunk, neck and other parts of the body. They are sometimes called 'voluntary muscles' because they produce the movements involved in activities such as walking, handling objects and participating in sports. It is important to note that these movements, which involve a very large number of brain processes as well as very many accurate muscle movements, are not really under any form of conscious control at all. When we carry out these functions, we are mainly conscious of the results we wish to achieve rather than the detailed means by which we attain the outcome. For example, we think 'I will pick up my keys' – we do not think 'I need to activate this muscle and then that one to direct my hand to the keys'.

The peripheral nerves

Muscles have two basic forms of nerve supply:

- efferent (motor) nerves, which carry messages *from* the brain to the muscle, and

- afferent (sensory) nerves, which carry information *to* the brain.

The efferent nerves activate systems which cause the muscle to contract with varying degrees of strength and speed, depending upon the type of message and the type of muscle fibre receiving the impulses. The impulses in the afferent nerves contain feedback information about the movement and position of the muscles and limbs, which the brain uses to ensure that the required movements are correctly carried out.

Feedback systems

In order to maintain and control appropriate body posture, the brain obtains information from a number of sources:

1. Information about body position from detectors in the muscles and ligaments. This is called *proprioceptive feedback*.

2. Signals from the eyes provide visual information about the environment and about body position. This is called *visual feedback*.

3. Signals from the semi-circular canals (vestibular system) near to the inner ear provide information about the body in relation to its environment and give it a 'sense of balance'. This is called *vestibular feedback*.

All the information provided by these feedback systems is continuously processed in the brain and it enables the brain to send appropriate instructions to the muscles to produce the highly coordinated movement patterns required for normal function.

Ligaments and tendons

Tendons are cable-like structures which connect muscles to the muscle attachments on bones. Ligaments are similar to tendons but attach bones to each other. It is generally agreed that the ligaments in people with Down syndrome are more elastic than in typically developing people.[see 10,11,12] The effect of having ligaments which are more stretchy than usual is that the

**DOWN SYNDROME
issues and
information**

joints are capable of a much greater range of movements than is typical. It is likely that this effect has been confused with that of muscle tone.

Change in performance over time

When children or adults begin to learn any new neuromuscular skill, such as walking, drawing or swimming, they initially carry out the task in a clumsy, not very well coordinated fashion. But, with sufficient practice, they will eventually perform the task in a smoother and more efficient manner. The effects of practice on the brain have been demonstrated in a number of studies.[see 5]

During the period when new types of coordinated movements are being learned, there may be some changes in the muscles involved, such as some increase in strength, but virtually all of the changes related to the development of the new skill take place in the brain. There is no evidence from the available research literature to indicate that factors associated with Down syndrome, such as shortened bone length, stretchy ligaments or altered muscle tone, have any significant effect on basic neuromuscular actions. Presumably this is because brain control systems compensate for these factors during the learning process.

Since muscles 'do what they are told', and since the instructions to the muscles all come from the brain, differences in the quality of movement such as slower or less well coordinated movement, can be seen to have their origin in the brain and, where changes in movement patterns occur, they are associated with changes in brain mechanisms.

Neuromotor programmes

Research has demonstrated that practice leads to learning and to the development of 'neuromotor programmes' or plans for particular movement sequences in the brain.[see 5,6] These neuromotor programmes enable movement sequences to be performed more quickly and accurately over time. As practice of the movement continues, the neuromotor programmes become so well learned that they are referred to as being 'automatised'. It has been suggested that, once neuromotor programmes are automatised, they make less demand on the information processing capacities of the brain.[6]

The effects of automatisation can be made clearer by considering a task in which a series of complex movements are learned, such as when learning to drive a car. In this situation the learner has to consciously control the series of movements – i.e. to think what to do next. However, over time, the series of actions may become so well practised and automatised that virtually no conscious control is needed to change gear or to steer the car. Now the driver can give more attention to road conditions and safety, as the conscious information processing demands of controlling the car have been considerably reduced.

Information processing and decision making

Subconscious processing

In all movements, there is a significant information processing requirement as the brain continuously processes feedback and sends control messages to the muscles in order to carry out the activity successfully, but this is at a subconscious level. The individual simply gets up and walks or picks up a cup without any conscious consideration of the controls on the movements needed for the particular situation – any conscious mental activity is simply focused on the goal of the activity.

Conscious processing

In addition, some motor tasks require conscious information processing and decision making before carrying out the movement. The 'reaction time' task used in research is one example, as a conscious level of decision making is involved before initiating the movement. The reaction time is the time taken between the signal to start a movement and the movement itself. Here, for example, a person may be instructed to tap the right button when the red light comes on or tap the left button when the green button comes on. He or she has to identify which light is on and then initiate the correct movement. Another example involving conscious processing of information before or during a movement is a physical education lesson, in which the pupil has to follow instructions.

Processing demands and processing abilities may vary

The information processing and the decision making requirements of a motor task influences an individual's speed and/or precision in carrying out the task. Some individuals may take more time to process information in the central nervous system and some may have more difficulty understanding task requirements or following instructions.

In summary

The production and co-ordination of movement comes from the central nervous system. Movements are controlled by the brain and practice leads to the establishment of learned neuromotor programmes, which increase the speed, accuracy and smoothness of movements. The brain focuses on the endpoint or goal of the activity and it controls the muscles to move the limbs to achieve that goal.[2] The brain gives instructions to the muscles that compensate for the effects of lax ligaments or muscle tone, or arm or finger length, when carrying out a movement.

Motor development from infancy

We have described some of the factors which influence all movements and in this section we consider the way in which motor skills develop during infancy amongst typically developing children.

Motor skills develop in a predictable sequence

There are many studies which have demonstrated that basic gross and fine motor skills usually develop in a specific order and which have documented the ages at which children sit, crawl, walk, jump, run, drink from a cup, use a knife to cut or a pen to write letters, manage buttons and zips. Specific gross and fine motor skills are assessed on many developmental tests, and motor skills also influence the scores of infants on some cognitive (mental) tests as they are expected to demonstrate their understanding by picking up or manipulating objects or toys during these tests.

Individual variation

As all parents know, the age at which healthy, typically developing children reach milestones can vary widely with some walking as early as 10 months and some as late as 24 months. This variation is largely thought to be determined by genetic make-up, but it is also affected by the opportunity to move

Movement in typical children

Motor skills develop in a predictable sequence.

There is individual variation in rates of progress.

Later skills are built on earlier skills.

All motor skills take time to develop to full competence.

All initial movements look clumsy and not well coordinated.

Change from clumsy and less precise to coordinated and precise is the result of practice.

Practice tends to increase muscle strength.

Practice develops better neurological coordination of movements.

Learned neuromotor programmes develop for specific movements.

The learned neuromotor programme becomes increasingly automatic (automatised).

Practice and automatisation lead to increasing speed as well as increasing smoothness and accuracy.

http://www.down-syndrome.info/library/dsii/12/01/
© Copyright 2003, The Down Syndrome Educational Trust. All Rights Reserved.
This page may not be reproduced without prior permission.

DOWN SYNDROME
issues and
information

and explore. For example, one Chinese study demonstrated later walking in those children kept in beds or cots for longer periods than usual because of living circumstances.[see 7]

Later skills tend to be built on earlier ones

The early gross motor skills of sitting, standing and walking involve increasingly successful control of body posture and balance, and these will be needed for maintaining body stability when bending to reach an object or later when writing and drawing, and when developing sporting skills.

All motor skills improve over time and with practice

This point has already been made, but it is worth emphasising. All children perform movements in a 'clumsy' or immature way at first and refine their performance with practice, often over many months or years. For example, for typical children, posture control when walking continues to improve up to at least 7 or 8 years of age.[8,9]

Practice improves the smoothness and accuracy of performance, the speed of performance and leads to automatisation of some of the processes.[6]

2. What do we know about the development of motor skills in children and adults with Down syndrome?

Research into the development of motor skills in children and adults with Down syndrome is limited at the present time.[10,11,12] The available research can be divided into two main types – descriptive studies and experimental studies.

Types of research

The studies of infants and children are mainly descriptive. Descriptive studies usually document the ages at which skills are attained. These may be basic gross and fine motor skills, and sometimes recreational skills as well as component skills such as balance, or hand-eye coordination. There have been a small number of experimental studies of children but most of the experimental work has examined the skills of teenagers and adults. Experimental studies usually require participants to learn a new motor action or to carry out actions at speed and then measure various aspects of their performance.

Limits of research

Unfortunately, the findings of many research studies in the area of motor skills have to be interpreted with caution for several reasons.

Small numbers. Researchers have often studied very small numbers of children or adults. For example, one widely quoted study reports findings based on 2 children with Down syndrome in one age group and 4 in another.[4] Given the considerable variability of progress among children and adults with Down syndrome, it is impossible to judge how representative the performance of such small numbers of children actually is, and therefore whether the findings can be generalised to all other children and adults with Down syndrome.

Date of studies. Some studies from the 1970s and 1980s will include children who grew up with low expectations, little or no early intervention support, and limited social and educational opportunities. Early studies may therefore be difficult to interpret.

Comparison groups. Another weakness of many studies lies in the comparison groups that they use. Many studies of both adults and children compare their motor skills with typically developing individuals of the same chronological age, usually reporting significant differences in performance, with those with Down syndrome having 'poorer' skills. However, when the comparison group is matched on mental age, then there are often no significant differences in the overall motor performance of the groups. Any differences that are found tend to reflect strength and balance issues or speed and accuracy of performance, rather than overall motor control. Examples of these findings are given in the relevant sections later in this overview.

Learning and practice effects. One problem that arises when the motor skills of children or adults with Down syndrome are compared with those of others is that it is difficult to control for their past experiences and the opportunities that they have had to develop their motor skills. They will usually have had less opportunity to practise than those they are being compared with. Practice improves motor skills until an optimal level of skill is achieved which does not improve further. In research studies, it is only possible to draw conclusions about differences in motor abilities if the participants are able to practise until they reach their peak performance, and there is evidence that individuals with Down syndrome require significantly more practice than others to reach their peak performance (see p.16).

Practical relevance. A number of studies are of theoretical rather than practical relevance. Currently many researchers are interested in the detailed way in which movements are carried out by individuals with Down syndrome and they measure differences in the angles of joint movements, take measures of the actual activation patterns of muscles, or study the differences in patterns of gait. Most of these studies indicate largely normal movement patterns.[13-16] Some do indicate difference in muscle activation patterns[5,15,17] or joint movements in experimental situations. However, since no one has conscious control over the sequence of actions of muscles or joints when moving, these studies have little direct practical relevance. It is also not clear from most of these studies whether these differences are developmental (i.e. seen in the early stages of learning a skill) and will disappear with practice.

Descriptive studies

The pattern of motor development for children and adults with Down syndrome

One of the important issues in the study of motor development in people with Down syndrome is whether there is delay in achieving milestones and/or whether movements are abnormal or not properly suited for their purpose. Some of the relevant research is considered in this section.

Development is the same but delayed

Motor development for children with Down syndrome is usually significantly delayed. All the basic motor skills are achieved by infants and children with Down syndrome in mostly the same order, but usually at significantly older ages when compared with typically developing infants and children. This is illustrated by the examples given in Table 1.

> **Motor development in children with Down syndrome**
>
> Motor skills develop in largely the same sequence as in typical children but later.
>
> They improve with practice – but may need more practice and take longer to improve.
>
> There is considerable individual variation in rates of progress.
>
> The majority of children with Down syndrome achieve all the basic skills necessary for everyday living and personal independence.
>
> Their fine motor skills steadily improve with practice and many can write, colour, draw and use a computer mouse and keyboard effectively.
>
> Achievements in recreational skills vary but often seem to reflect family enthusiasms. Some children become very competent swimmers, skiers or gymnasts for example.
>
> Most research suggests that their motor skills are similar to typically developing children of similar general mental ability (therefore younger).
>
> However, balance seems to be a particular difficulty relative to progress in general coordination and muscle strength.

DOWN SYNDROME
**issues and
information**

Table I: Motor Milestones - A guide to ages of attainment for children with Down syndrome

Attainment	Cunningham & Sloper[18]		Berry et al[19]	Winders[20]	Typical development	
	Range	Average age (months)	Range	Average age (months)	Range	Average age (months)
Rolls	4 to 11	8	2 to 12	6 - 7	2 to 10	5
Sits steadily without support	8 to 16	11	7 to 16	11	5 to 9	7
Pulls to standing	10 to 24	17	8 to >28	17	7 to 12	8
Stands alone	16 to 36	22	–	21	9 to 16	11
Walks without support 3 steps or more	16 to 42	24	14 to 36	26	9 to 17	13
Grasps cube	4 to 10	7	–	–	3 to 7	5
Passes object from hand to hand	6 to 12	8	–	–	4 to 8	5
Puts 3 or more objects into cup/box	12 to 34	19	–	–	9 to 18	12
Builds a tower of two 1" cubes	14 to 32	20	–	–	10 to 19	14

There is evidence that some motor skills, such as those requiring fine finger to thumb opposition position (pincer grasp) and those requiring fine control of balance, may be achieved later than is typical and therefore slightly out of the usual sequence. One study of 220 young children with Down syndrome aged 3 months to 60 months[21] assessed their progress on specific gross and fine motor skills on the Bayley Scales of Infant Development. This test provides norms for the ages and expected sequence of the achievement of early motor skills in typically developing children. This study found that picking up tiny objects, walking backwards, standing on one foot, jumping and walking downstairs without support, were all achieved later than is typical, and late in relation to other motor skills. The reader may note that standing and walking were not relatively delayed, in fact both standing and walking 10 feet on tiptoes were achieved relatively early in the sequence. It seems that it is skills requiring more complex balance control that are achieved later. Balance is discussed more fully in the next section.

There is increased variability

There is greater variability in the basic motor progress of children with Down syndrome when compared with typically developing children. For example, the average age for walking in typically developing children is 13 months and the range is 9-17 months, while the average age for walking in children with Down syndrome is 24 months and the range is 14-42 months. Some of this greater variability may reflect the effects of health status for some children. Children with major heart abnormalities may be slower to achieve some motor milestones until they have corrective surgery, and the minority who cannot have corrective surgery will continue to be delayed. Similarly, a small number of children with Down syndrome have additional brain damage and will be more severely delayed in their motor progress. We need to study the progress of large numbers of children and take account of their health status, in order to develop sufficiently detailed data to enable parents and practitioners to accurately predict the progress to be expected of individual children.

Guides to expected progress

The figures provided in Table 2 may be a useful general guide to expected progress. They are based on a study of the gross motor progress of 121 Canadian children with Down syndrome aged 1 month to 6 years.[22] The figures give the percentage of children who have achieved a skill at each chronological age point. The researchers in this study found that the children's rate of progress slowed between the ages

Table 2: The percentage of children with Down syndrome achieving skills at each age point. Adapted with permission from Elsevier [22 p.499]

Milestone	Age (months)								
	6	**12**	**18**	**24**	**30**	**36**	**48**	**60**	**72**
Rolling	51	64	74	83	89	93	97	99	100
Sitting	8	78	99	100	100	100	100	100	100
Crawling	10	19	34	53	71	84	96	99	100
Standing	4	14	40	73	91	98	100	100	100
Walking	1	4	14	40	74	92	99	100	100
Running	1	2	3	5	8	12	25	45	67
Climbing step	0	0	1	1	3	5	18	46	77
Jumping forward	0	0	0	1	2	5	18	52	84

of 3 and 6 years when they were learning to run, jump and climb stairs, confirming the findings of other studies that as the balance, speed and coordination requirements of movements increase, the children have relatively greater difficulty. However, these researchers also stress that while having Down syndrome did affect the rate at which new skills were mastered, it did not affect the upper limit of the skills achieved – most children can run, climb steps and jump by 6 to 7 years. It takes children with Down syndrome longer to reach a milestone and longer to refine and improve movements but, with enough practice and encouragement, they will achieve it.

Progress in teenage years

There is only one study reporting in detail on the motor progress of older children with Down syndrome and this does not provide any normative data for the achievement of particular scores but it does illustrate continued improvement for most children on most skills from 10 to 16 years.[23,24] In this study, information on the fine and gross motor skill development of 105 Australian children was studied over a number of years. The children were assessed at regular intervals on the Bruininks Oseretsky Test of Motor Proficiency (BOTMP) which has 8 subtests designed to assess:-

1. Running speed and agility – the speed with which a child can run 13.7 metres, pick up an object and return to the start.

2. Balance – a number of balance items such as standing on one leg with eyes open and closed.

3. Bilateral coordination – a number of items requiring different limbs to be temporally coordinated e.g synchronised tapping of the right finger and left foot or right finger and right foot.

4. Strength – tasks requiring strength, including sit-ups and push-ups.

5. Upper-limb coordination – items exploring ball skill and manual dexterity (e.g. finger/thumb opposition).

DOWN SYNDROME
issues and
information

6. Response speed – reaction times to a simple stimulus.

7. Visual-motor control – items involving cutting, drawing and copying, without being timed.

8. Upper-limb dexterity – items needing a sequence of manual movements e.g. posting coins through a slot, and requiring tasks to be completed within a time limit.

The BOTMP provides norms for the typical ages at which specific levels of performance on the tasks will be achieved and age-related scores can be computed for each of the 8 skill areas.

On all the skill areas the group showed some progress between 10 and 16 years. There was considerable individual variability and the rate of the children's progress was largely predicted by their mental age, rather than chronological age. While there was a close link between mental and motor age, with those with higher mental age scores tending to have higher motor age scores, on most motor subtests the group had significantly higher mean ages for motor skills. All the subtests scores are higher except for balance, which is lower, and response speed, which is at the level expected for mental age. It is difficult to know how to interpret these findings, as it is always difficult to draw firm conclusions when comparing age-equivalent scores in different areas of development when the tests used have been standardised on different groups of children at different times.

Looking at a subgroup of 16 boys and 13 girls for whom consistent longitudinal data was available, the boys scored higher than girls on running speed and agility, strength, and upper-limb coordination. While a number of the teenagers were reported to be overweight (the Body Mass Index Scores were analysed for the whole group), there was no measurable link between being overweight and motor skill achievements on the BOTMP tests at this early stage of adolescence.

Clumsiness and refinement of movements

Some authors observe that many movements continue to seem somewhat 'clumsy' in individuals with Down syndrome.[5] It takes them longer to improve their skills and they may not reach quite the same levels of fine coordination that most of us take for granted, but the levels they do achieve will usually be adequate for successful performance. Improvements in basic fine motor skills such as tying a shoelace or writing often continue to improve through early adult life. However, it is important to stress the wide variability in progress again, as many children and adults with Down syndrome do not seem at all 'clumsy' when walking, running, picking up a cup, writing, skiing, skateboarding or doing gymnastics. The final level of co-ordination and skill achieved seems to have much to do with encouragement and opportunities to take up sports and to practice. We know many individuals who have achieved high levels of competence in basic, recreational and employment skills, and therefore we should never assume that having Down syndrome necessarily puts an upper limit on what a particular individual may achieve.

More difficulty with balance and strength

A number of studies [2,9,13] indicate that balance is a particular difficulty and continues to be a weakness in teenage years.[23,24] This may explain why many young people with Down syndrome find riding a bicycle rather difficult to master. Some children do become competent on two wheels but many do not achieve this, although they may be very competent on a tricycle. In a recent study of a representative group of teenagers conducted by the authors, 93% could ride a tricycle and 36% could ride a bicycle.[44]

Strength also tends to be less even when the comparison is with young people of similar age and general mental abilities.[25,26] The explanation for this is not clear. Everyone increases their muscle strength through active movement and it could be that individuals with Down syndrome engage in less active movement, although there is no direct evidence of this. The babies, toddlers and children that we see regularly in our preschool and school services seem to us to be quite active. It could be that children with Down syndrome need more exercise to reach the same levels of strength. This is another area where we know from our practical experience that there are considerable individual differences, with some teenagers with Down syndrome being as strong or stronger than their non-disabled peer group in school. Teenagers who do gymnastics, karate or weightlifting, for example, can be as strong as non-disabled peers, so again, having Down syndrome *per se* does not impose upper limits on strength.

Experimental studies of movement skills

Studies which compare children or adults with Down syndrome with typically developing individuals of the same age almost always report differences or delays. These comparisons are of limited value as we need to know if these differences simply reflect developmental immaturity – that is, are the individuals with Down syndrome carrying out the task as a younger person of similar mental age would? This is the only way to identify any differences which would have a practical implication for therapy or teaching approaches. We have focused, therefore, on reporting studies that include mental age matched comparison groups and discuss some representative examples of these studies.

Laboratory studies of basic skills

Some experimental studies have looked in detail at the way in which basic skills such as reaching and grasping or walking are carried out by children and adults with Down syndrome, others have studied the ways in which they perform experimental movement tasks.

Reaching and grasping. In a study of reaching and grasping – the movements used throughout the day to handle objects, the skills of 12 children aged 8 to 10 years with Down syndrome were compared with two groups of typically developing children, one of the same age and one younger and mental age matched.[16] The researchers report that the performance of the children with Down syndrome was essentially the same as that of the younger children. They performed the tasks at the same speed and showed the same ability to adjust their grasps for the size of the object to be picked up as the younger children. They mostly showed the same use of a pincer grip, although 2 children with Down syndrome had unusual grasps, with a tendency to use the palm and all their fingers, rather than finger and thumb. There was more variability in the movement patterns, and a little less accuracy, which the researchers suggest indicates that more practice would be needed to establish more effective motor patterns. Overall, the study indicated that reaching and grasping were delayed rather than different. Similar findings, indicating the ability to adjust to the size of the object, are reported in another study of grasping in 4 to 11 year olds with Down syndrome.[40]

**DOWN SYNDROME
issues and
information**

Walking. In a study of the walking patterns of children and adults with Down syndrome, 5 children aged 4 to 9 years and 3 adults of 30 to 38 years were compared with a typical adult of 22 years on several tasks, walking and running in bare feet on a hard floor, walking on the elastic surface of a trampoline and walking on a narrow beam. The researchers report [13 p.79,80] that the walking patterns of the children with Down syndrome on a hard floor were very similar to those of the adults with Down syndrome and the typical adult. The movements of their joints are described as showing 'very smooth trajectories' and to 'resemble adult patterns of walking'. The children and adults with Down syndrome also showed patterns of co-ordination similar to that of the typical adult when running. There was some evidence of differences in the precise details of the range of joint and limb movements but the overall picture was of effective, smooth and largely normal movement. As this study does not include any mental age matched children or adults for comparison, any reported differences may only indicate immaturity at this point. On the trampoline and the balance surfaces, the children and adults with Down syndrome had more difficulty. Both tasks require more skill in balance and they were less able to manage these tasks competently than the typical adult. The changes that they showed in their knee movements and step lengths were attempts to compensate for balance difficulties. Here again, with no mental age comparison and small numbers, the significance of these patterns cannot be interpreted. They could indicate ongoing difficulties with balance, and/or delayed progress.

Laboratory studies of specific movements

Slower reaction times

When teenagers and adults with Down syndrome are asked to perform motor tasks in experimental situations, such as tapping a particular button when a particular light comes on, their reaction times have been reported as slower than those of typical individuals of the same age and the same when compared with mental age matched controls.[see 14,15] However, in some studies there is a difference in reaction times for people with Down syndrome when instructions are visual rather than verbal. They show faster reaction times when instructions are visual and show significantly slower reaction times when the instructions are verbal. In everyday life, reaction times influence the speed of starting a movement from the time an instruction is given, for example, at the start of a race.

Slower movement times

Some studies have reported slower times (compared with mental age matched groups) for the movement component of tasks as well as the reaction time.[14,15] The movement time is the time taken from the initiation of the movement to reaching the end point of the movement – for example, the time taken from initiating the movement to completing the tap in the reaction time task. Individuals with Down syndrome show slower movement times on experimental tasks when instructions are verbal, but when instructions were visual, their performance was the same as mental age matched peers.[see 14] One research group suggests that this indicates a specific verbal-motor impairment in individuals with Down syndrome and that this may reflect different brain organisation for movement control,[27] but this hypothesis needs more research.

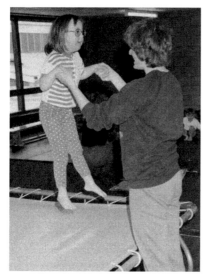

Learning specific movements in experimental situations

When learning new movements and being expected to be as fast and accurate as possible, in comparison with others of a similar mental or general functional age, individuals with Down syndrome are usually:-
- Slower to react and initiate a movement
- Slower to complete a movement
- More accurate - make fewer errors

In addition:-
- Their reaction times improve with practice
- They perform better when instructions are visual rather than verbal

Delayed but visual learners

Overall, this group of leading movement researchers identify that research studies consistently show that the development of motor skills of individuals with Down syndrome is essentially delayed rather than different. It is linked to progress in general mental age and progresses in a typical but slower way, except for the specific difficulty in processing verbal instructions. They conclude therefore that *"a developmental model of information processing and skill acquisition should be used to guide the instructional protocols used by clinicians, teachers and parents attempting to optimise skilled perform-ance".*[14 p. 67] The advice to use a 'developmental model' means that parents and teachers should expect movements to be achieved and improved in the same way as they are in typically developing children and adults, although more slowly. Teaching activities should, therefore, be those appropriate for the stage of movement skill that a child or adult has achieved. The practical implications of the verbal instruction findings are that, within a developmen-tal framework, instructions for motor activities of all kinds, from writing to dancing, should be by modelling or demonstrating actions whenever possible. There are, in fact, studies showing that the motor areas of the brain which control movement are activated by passively watching a movement, which may partially explain the advantage of learning by watching, rather than by verbal instruction.[45]

Practice improves performance

Data from experimental studies requiring fine motor tasks to be carried out [6,15] and from real life studies of activities such as running,[28] report sig-nificant improvement in the performance of tasks with practice – improve-ments in both speed and accuracy of movements. For example, a group of adolescents with Down syndrome enrolled in a physical training programme showed considerable improvements as a result of training. The mean time to run the 50 metre dash dropped from 15.39 to 10.69 seconds. However, some of these studies concluded that individuals with Down syn-drome require about twice as much practice to reach the same level as typically developing individuals of the same mental age.[28] They seem to need more practice to establish motor programmes.

The positive effects of practice are well illustrated in a series of studies[29-31] in which the researchers compared the performance of 10 adolescents with Down syndrome, average age 16 years, with that of 3 other groups of stu-dents; one group of the same age with learning disabilities but not Down syndrome, one group of typically develop-ing high school students of the same age and one group of younger typically developing children of the same devel-opmental age. The young people were asked to perform a pursuit–tracking task (see Figure 2) which requires them to move the pointer to the target light. The pointer is moved by turning the steering wheel and once the pointer has been on that target light for 200 milliseconds, the light goes off and another comes on. The pointer then has to be moved to that light. In one trial of 100 moves, the lights come on in a pattern that requires 50 moves to the right and 50 moves to the left. The probability of moving in a particular direction

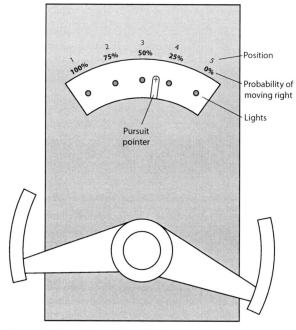

Figure 2. Pursuit tracking device

DOWN SYNDROME
issues and
information

varies according to current position, as illustrated in Figure 2. If the pointer is on the far left light, there will be 100% probability that the next required move will be to the right and if the pointer is on the middle light, the probability of moving right or left is the same – 50%. The probabilities for each light are illustrated in the figure. In the studies, the researchers were interested in the speed (measuring both reaction time and movement time) and accuracy with which the young people could carry out the task, and whether they used the probability information to improve their performance.

Speed and accuracy

In the first study,[29] the young people carried out 8 trials comprising 800 actual moves of the pointer. The young people with Down syndrome scored at the same level on reaction times as their peers with learning disabilities and both these groups were slower than the typically developing high school and elementary school students. On movement times the pattern was the same. However, on accuracy, the young people with Down syndrome were significantly better than all the other groups – therefore they were even more accurate than non-disabled peers of the same chronological age. They were slower than their non-disabled peer group but they made fewer errors. The mean error rate for the group with Down syndrome was 8%, and for the learning disabled and high school groups 13%. However, the young people with Down syndrome did not show any evidence of making use of probability data, that is, they did not react faster when it was possible to predict the likely direction of movement, although the other groups were able to do this.

Reaction times improve with practice

These researchers went on to extend this work[31] and in another study using the same groups and design, they increased the amount of practice to 24 trials and, therefore, 2400 moves. For reaction times, again, the typically developing high school students were faster, but the other 3 groups were not different from one another – that is, the young people with Down syndrome were as fast as the younger typically developing children and their peers with learning disabilities. This time, having been given much more practice at the task, the young people with Down syndrome did show evidence of using probability information when reaction times were analysed to take account of this, i.e. the more predictable the direction to move in for the next light the faster their reaction time. However, their reaction times continued to be longer for longer movements, and this is not easy to interpret.

Slower but more accurate

For movement times, the young people with Down syndrome were slower than all the other groups but again, they were more accurate – they made fewer errors than all the other groups.

When given sufficient training, the young people with Down syndrome significantly reduced their reaction times – they were about 36% faster in reacting and initiating movements, but they did not improve their movement times. They seemed to focus on accuracy and were unwilling to increase speed. This is entirely sensible as, in all studies looking at speed and accuracy on this sort of task, there is a link or 'trade-off' as a point is reached where it is not possible to improve one without a negative effect on the other; after this level of performance has been reached, an increase in speed leads to a decrease in accuracy (this is called Fitt's Law).

http://www.down-syndrome.info/library/dsii/12/01/

Individual differences

Within the group of 24 young people with Down syndrome who took part in one of the studies[30] using this task, the performance of individuals tended to be linked to general mental age, that is, those with higher mental ages did better on the tasks than those with lower mental ages.

The importance of practice

These general findings of improvement with practice, slower movement speeds and a focus on accuracy rather than speed have been confirmed in other studies.[see 15] Many studies indicate that teenagers and adults show considerable improvement with practice. This indicates that they have not yet reached their optimal levels of performance, possibly because they have not had enough opportunity to practise both gross and fine motor skills during childhood. In some studies, their performance after practice is as good as typically developing individuals of the same age.[5,43]

Why this profile of development?

At the present time, we do not have enough knowledge about the reasons for these features of motor development in individuals with Down syndrome but we do have several facts which may provide some clues and guidance for more effective intervention.

Closely linked to mental age

Both the descriptive studies of children's progress and some experimental studies of motor skills in adults identify that the motor performance of individuals with Down syndrome is closely linked to their general cognitive progress. In other words, for gross motor, fine motor and experimental tasks, they usually perform like other children or adults with the same cognitive or mental age. This suggests that the main effect is delay rather than difference in motor progress.

Early childhood. The close relationship between early mental and motor development is illustrated in the graphs in Figure 3. These graphs are based on 707 assessments of 220 children on the Bayley Scales of Infant Development.[32] A team of researchers pooled the data collected on children in Australia, Canada and Germany and some of the children had been assessed several times at different ages as they were involved in on-going longitudinal studies. This provided some 707 separate assessments covering the chronological age range from 3 months to 54 months. The reader can see that the group is progressing at a very similar rate in mental and motor development. The correspondence is exceptionally close at this age range and studies of older children show that the relationship holds into the teenage years.

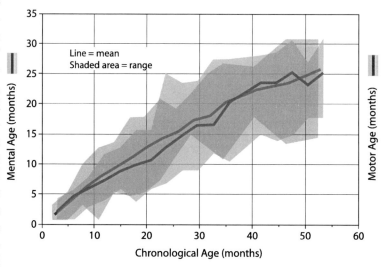

Figure 3. Mental and motor progress in children with Down syndrome (Adapted from [32, p.339] with permission)

DOWN SYNDROME issues and information

Later childhood. One American study charted the progress of 15 children with Down syndrome who were 7 to 10 years of age, and who had had the advantage of well-organised early intervention and education. The findings in Table 3 show the close relationship between their mental and motor progress. For the reader interested in the data, the correlations between the fine motor and gross motor skills and mental age are both .64 and statistically highly significant.[33] A study of 99 Australian 10 to 16 year olds with Down syndrome also showed the close link between motor skills and mental age, with the children's mental age rather than their chronological age, predicting performance and progress.[23,24]

Table 3: Relationship between mental and motor progress in children with Down syndrome

Based on data published in [33, Table 2, p.1317]

	Range	Mean
Mental age	3y 3m - 6y 8m	4y 8m
Gross motor age	3y 5m - 6y 0m	4y 9m
Fine motor age	4y 2m - 6y 2m	4y 10m

(The fine motor scores are based on 12 children, as three children with mental ages between 3 years 3 months to 3 years 9 months were not tested on the fine motor scale.)

The reason for the close association of overall mental and motor development is not clear, but it may reflect that the control of motor skills is largely a central nervous system activity and that brain functions play a central role in motor development in the same way as they do in other aspects of development. It could be that both mental and motor development are delayed by similar differences in brain processes. One of these differences could be speed of information processing in the brain. Another could be the ability to establish learned programmes in the brain. A number of studies have highlighted the inconsistent performance of children with Down syndrome on both cognitive and language tasks. It seems to take them longer (i.e. they need more practice) to effectively consolidate new learning.[34]

Individual variability

The reader should note that the close link between the development of mental and motor skills indicated in these studies does not mean that this close correspondence will apply to every individual child at any particular stage. For example, a particular three year old with Down syndrome may be making rapid progress with language but still not be walking, another three year old may show the opposite profile, walking but not yet talking. The overall mental and motor age scores used in these studies are each based on a large number of tasks to give an overall picture of mental and motor development and there will be variability in the way individual children achieve their overall scores. However, the link between overall mental age and progress in overall motor skills is a powerful trend in all studies that have looked at both, and is clearly of significance in understanding the issues.

More dependent on visual feedback

Researchers have reported that children and adults with Down syndrome rely more on visual feedback while carrying out a task than typically developing individuals.[see 9,35] They may need to rely to a greater extent on visual feedback because they take much longer to establish learned motor programmes for the task. This can make their performance seem as if they are tackling each repetition of the task as if they have not performed it before. It also means that their pattern of movement may be jerky and inconsistent from one time to the next even though they can actually perform the task correctly. This finding could explain longer movement times because, as a learned programme is established, the sequence of movements required for a movement can be performed more quickly.

Balance

As already identified, there is some evidence that balance may be a particular difficulty for individuals with Down syndrome. In one experimental study, the balancing abilities of infants with Down syndrome were compared with typically developing infants and the two groups were carefully matched for their ability to stand unsupported.[9] The infants were put into a small room in which the floor was stable but the walls could be moved to give the impression of the room tilting. All the infants reacted as if the floor was also tilting by leaning, swaying, staggering or falling, that is, they reacted as if to stop themselves from falling even though the floor they were standing on did not move. The visual information suggested they were being tilted even though the vestibular and proprioceptive feedback would not have suggested this.

The children with Down syndrome were more affected and made larger postural adjustments than the typically developing children. Both groups of children improved as they increased their experience of walking and after some 12 months of walking the typically developing children were finally able to stay stable in the tilting room and not react to the false visual cues. The children with Down syndrome needed longer to become stable and did not show complete stability after a year or more of walking experience, even though they were improving. The authors suggest that these findings indicate that children with Down syndrome are more dependent on visual cues to judge body position than typically developing children at the same stage of walking, because they need extra visual information to compensate for less effective vestibular and proprioceptive feedback at this stage.

Another similar study of 26 older children with Down syndrome (mean age 10.6 years) showed that they were still more affected by this kind of experience and showed more body sway than other children of the same age. [41]

There is other evidence to suggest that balance continues to be an area of specific difficulty into the teenage years. In an Australian study of the motor skills of 81 twelve year olds,[23,24] balance was the weakest area and still at a 4 year level when their other motor skills range from 5 to 9 year levels. Their mean mental age was 4 years 9 months and therefore most of the motor skills for the group were higher than might be expected, with response speed at the same level as mental age and only balance lower than mental age. There was considerable variability in motor skills between individuals and, as in other studies, mental and motor skills were related. Individuals with lower mental ages tended to have lower motor skill scores, and vice versa.

Physical differences

Many authors assume that the profile of motor development in Down syndrome is largely the result of physical differences, but the evidence for this point of view is limited. Almost every discussion of motor development in children with Down syndrome starts with descriptions of hypotonia and lax ligaments, and suggests that they are to blame for the motor delays.

Hypotonia and lax ligaments

Many newborn children with Down syndrome have very flaccid muscles and are described as 'floppy'. There are many specific disorders which are associated with the birth of 'floppy' infants; in some cases this disappears as the child develops and in some cases they remain in this 'floppy' state. There

---

The significance of hypotonia

At birth, babies with Down syndrome are observed to be more 'floppy' than other babies.

This has been described as hypotonia but there is no agreed definition of hypotonia.

There seems to be evidence for:-

- lower muscle 'tone', defined as either less resistance to passive movement or feel softer if pressed – both unsatisfactory as there are no precise measures and no comparisons with mental age matched infants without disabilities.
- 'lax ligaments', implied by the fact that limbs can be more widely rotated – there is more movement in the joints allowing children to take up unusual postures such as widely splayed hips when moving on floor or sitting.

Both muscle 'tone' and 'lax ligaments' improve with age and with movement.

There is no convincing evidence that these factors affect movement ability, i.e. the brain may be compensating for them when child moves.

However, it has been suggested that they may affect the development of movements if child takes up odd postures or tries to move limbs differently in the early stages of learning a movement – studies are needed on this issue.

DOWN SYNDROME
issues and
information

are a few follow up studies of infants with Down syndrome and it seems that this infant floppiness does improve over time. There is a fairly widespread belief that the children remain with a degree of hypotonia and this state is often invoked as being responsible for much of the 'poor' motor function seen in people with Down syndrome.

However, this is a rather controversial issue since there is no proper agreement as to the definition of hypotonia and there is no consensus as to how to measure it. In addition, some recent studies have demonstrated that the hypotonia seen when children and adults with Down syndrome are not moving (i.e. their tendency to have more 'floppy' muscles at rest) is not evident when they are moving and does not actually impair coordinated movement.[see 8,15]

It is generally accepted that ligaments and tendons in individuals with Down syndrome are more 'stretchy' than is usual. This would explain why they are often able to move their joints into extreme positions. However, research indicates that this does not prevent coordinated control of the joints to perform ordinary movements.[8,15] Both muscle 'tone' and 'lax ligaments' improve with age and with movement, and there is no convincing evidence that these factors affect the development of movements, i.e. the brain is likely to be compensating for them as the child moves.

Clearly, a great deal of research needs to be done to clarify the different contributions of the stretchiness of ligaments and tendons, the strength of the muscles, the 'tone' of the muscles and the contribution of the nervous input to the greater picture of motor function in individuals with Down syndrome.

Health issues

Some authors rightly draw attention to a number of medical conditions that are more common in individuals with Down syndrome and which may affect a child's or adult's ability to be active, if not effectively treated.[10,11,36] These include heart conditions, underactive thyroid function, vision and hearing issues, atlanto-axial instability and obesity. It will be important to take account of health factors for individual children and adults when considering active sports but most will not prevent progress in basic gross or fine motor skills. The relevance of each of these illness conditions for activity will be the same as it is in the rest of the population. Parents and carers are likely to know about their children's medical and healthcare needs and will inform teachers and therapists. Some authors also draw attention to the tendency for individuals with Down syndrome to have small stature and small hands relative to typically developing individuals. However many, if not most, have similar stature to those at the small end of the general population and the restrictions this imposes on achievements in sports will be the same for both groups. More information on health issues for children with Down syndrome can be found in each age-specific overview in the DSii series – see Resources list.

In summary

The movement skills of children with Down syndrome are largely delayed rather than different and progress at the same pace as their general mental development. They may take longer and need more practice to improve their performance and they may continue to have more difficulty with tasks requiring balance. Most children achieve competence in all everyday gross and fine motor skills even though they develop more slowly. Despite the presence of lax ligaments and possible hypotonia, there is little evidence that they impair controlled movements as the central nervous system controls all movement and usually compensates for such variables.

Teenagers and adults with Down syndrome may be slower to perform movements in some situations, possibly reflecting slower information processing in the central nervous system and/or a focus on accuracy and safe, effective movements rather than on speed.[5]

3. What do we know about the effects of interventions?

Interventions for basic skills

There are very few evaluations of therapy aimed at improving or accelerating the development of basic skills for children with Down syndrome.[10] Some early intervention programmes which target all aspects of development indicate gains in motor development with milestones reached earlier.[33] This may be because babies are encouraged to be more active and interested in their environment, and encouraged to play and to move.

One evaluation of a typical physiotherapy programme reported no significant gains in motor development for infants with Down syndrome in therapy compared with infants not receiving therapy.[37] Another recent study evaluated a very specific therapy to encourage walking by supporting infants with Down syndrome to walk on a treadmill for up to 8 minutes a day from the time that they could sit without support.[38] The treadmill infants walked on average 101 days earlier than a comparison group, presumably as a result of this increased practice. Being able to practise walking while supported upright on the treadmill presumably gave the infants the opportunity to increase muscle strength and to develop their balance. The practice may also have helped them to develop a neuromotor programme for walking.

We found no evaluations of the adaptations and advice offered to improve gross or fine motor skills for children with Down syndrome. However, many practical aids such as the appropriate size of chair and table, special grips for spoons, pens and pencils, and spring loaded scissors may be helpful in giving a child improved opportunities to practise. In addition, many practical programmes provide ideas for activities which will encourage a child to practise.

Activities designed to increase muscle strength of the whole body and of the hands are likely to be beneficial, as are activities that will improve balance such as walking on a beam (at ground level), hopping, and playing football.

This lack of research evidence does not, of course, mean that babies and children with Down syndrome do not necessarily benefit from the recommendations given in books of practical advice – we do not know because the studies have not been done. However, the benefits are likely to be mainly the result of providing games and activities which encourage and increase active movement therefore increasing the child's amount of practice. Practice allows the central nervous system to develop more effective neuromotor programmes for smoother and more coordinated movement.

See also:

- *An overview of the development of infants with Down syndrome (0-5 years) [DSii-01-02]*
- *An overview of the development of children with Down syndrome (5-11 years) [DSii-01-04]*
- *An overview of the development of teenagers with Down syndrome (11-16 years) [DSii-01-06]*

DOWN SYNDROME issues and information

Interventions for recreational skills

We also found no data on the numbers of teenagers or adults with Down syndrome who become competent in recreational skills, or any studies documenting the effects of teaching such skills to a representative group. There are a few studies indicating both improvement in performance, and in strength and fitness, from athletics training[28] and fitness training[42] programmes similar to those offered to typically developing children and adults. There are a number of articles and chapters encouraging educators to improve the opportunities for children, teenagers and adults to enjoy a wide range of sporting and recreational activities and identifying the social and health benefits. We would entirely agree with this advice, as it applies to everyone, but we would benefit from more information on successful programmes and some actual measurement of the benefits.

Preventing abnormalities

Some physiotherapists suggest that the main aim of therapy in infancy is to prevent abnormal postures and gait[39] which may be the result of lax ligaments, such as widely splayed hips when sitting, a wide based gait or turning the feet out when walking. However, some of the most knowledgeable current researchers in the area argue that 'abnormalities' in the way movements are carried out may be necessary adaptations at particular stages, for example, to enable children to maintain their balance.[5,17] They argue that the movement seen may be the most effective adaptation the child or adult can make at a particular stage of development and that we should not be trying to push them towards 'normal' postures and styles of movement.

One concern we have is that therapy may not always seem to take account of the child's developmental stage – the child with Down syndrome may be showing immature styles of movement that are seen in younger children when they begin to use the same movements. In addition, because children with Down syndrome progress more slowly, they may use immature styles for longer and need more practice to improve and gain better control and coordination.

We also have concerns about supportive aids that restrict movement, as they may prevent the child from being able to control the restricted joint and muscles. This prevents the practice of effective control of the movement and it will prevent gains in muscle strength. However, at the same time, we do not know if any lasting harm comes from continuing to use 'abnormal' movements, such as crab crawling with the knees out sideways to the body and hips rotated. It has been suggested that this may lead to long term damage of hip joints but no one actually knows if this is true as there are no long term follow up studies. The body is a dynamic and flexible system and it is quite possible that no harm comes from these actions in the long term.

In summary

It seems that we have no real evidence that interventions other than encouraging and increasing the opportunities for active movement influence motor progress.

4. Implications for effective intervention

Research studies at the present time indicate that motor development is essentially delayed in children with Down syndrome and generally proceeds at a similar pace to their mental development. This may indicate that they take longer to manage the information processing demands of controlled movement and to establish learned neuromotor programmes for movement.

There are two main implications of these findings:

- The most effective way to develop any controlled movement is to actually practise the movement.

- More practice will be needed to improve movements.

Some experts suggest that individuals with Down syndrome may actually avoid practising some motor skills, if they fear that they will have difficulty. This might particularly apply to activities which involve movement and balance, such as running, jumping, trampolining or balancing on a beam, but it could also apply to everyday tasks, such as carrying a cup full of liquid or a plate of food, pouring out drinks, or trying to fasten coats and shoes. One author[5] emphasises the need to encourage the practice of movements in varying conditions, to encourage individuals to reach optimal levels of skill. Examples of this approach could be encouraging walking or running on hard surfaces, grass, sand, pebbles or foam mats, encouraging games with different size balls to catch or to kick, and encouraging the practice of pouring with jugs or containers and cups of different sizes.

In addition, research studies indicate that balance may be a specific difficulty relative to progress in other aspects of movement skills. This suggests that:

- practising activities requiring balance will be beneficial.

Some studies suggest that low muscle strength may also delay progress although strength may, in fact, be appropriate when developmental age is taken into account. However:

- specific exercises to improve muscle strength may be beneficial, although all physical activities will increase strength to some degree.

Studies also suggest that children and adults with Down syndrome are visual learners, therefore:

- remember to demonstrate or model all activities.

In the next section, we offer some key guidelines for developing both basic and recreational skills. More detailed advice and suggestions for activities are contained in the age-specific practical motor skills books in this series.

Developing basic skills

Encourage active movement

Since the most important factor in improving movement is the control from the brain, it is important to find fun ways to encourage infants and children to initiate their own movements. This applies to babies and toddlers when learning all the basic skills such as rolling, reaching, grasping, sitting, standing, walking and feeding. All babies learn through play, and play provides many opportunities to develop and improve gross and fine motor skills.

What are the implications for intervention?

The most effective way to improve all types of movement is practice.

Children with Down syndrome need more practice to improve movements than other children.

Help infants to practice activities that need strength and balance such as sitting and walking by providing supports for practice.

Compensate for the social and cognitive effects of late movement.

Encourage as much active movement as possible in natural ways through play and activities such as swimming, gymnastics and games in the park.

Teach by visually demonstrating or modelling the actions.

Start to encourage an interest in sports as early as possible.

Teenagers and adults will benefit from activities to improve strength and balance.

It is never too late - many adults take up new recreational activities and continue to develop basic skills in their 20s and 30s.

See also:

- *Motor skills development for infants with Down syndrome (0-5 years)* [DSii-12-02]
- *Motor skills development for children with Down syndrome (5-11 years)* [DSii-12-03]
- *Motor skills development for teenagers with Down syndrome (11-16 years)* [DSii-12-04]

DOWN SYNDROME
issues and
information

Encourage practice

Fun activities need to be encouraged as often as possible to give the child practice. Some activities, such as walking, may need support. When babies bounce on their parents' knees, they are strengthening their legs with the help of support before they can stand. Gaining balance and posture control for walking seems to take quite a while, and practice in walking with a truck to push or supervised practice for short periods in a baby-walker may be beneficial. Baby bouncers will also strengthen the legs if used for brief, supervised sessions. We know that many professionals advise against these aids, but if they are used wisely they can increase the child's opportunity to practise walking, as the treadmill study did.

Choose activities to help balance and strength

All active movement will improve balance and strength, but it is also possible to think of particular activities to target one or the other. Supervised trampolining will improve balance and strength, for example, as will skipping, hopping, jumping and kicking a ball. Hand gym exercises (e.g. squeezing balls of different textures or moulding playdoh) will improve hand strength.

Teach by modelling

Movement research indicates that it is more effective to teach children with Down syndrome by modelling (visually demonstrating) the activity than by giving verbal instructions. This suggests that children will learn more effectively by being able to imitate or copy actions. They have strengths as visual learners in all areas of their development.

Encourage fine motor skills

It is important to encourage all fine motor skills – initially through play, feeding and dressing. In later childhood, encourage mastery of skills useful in the kitchen such as pouring, cutting, and spreading, and personal care skills such as managing fastenings, including laces, and using scissors or clippers for cutting nails. The authors' surveys of teenage development suggest that parents often continue to provide too much help with daily tasks rather than to encourage practice of these skills.[44] While many young people take time to develop writing and drawing skills, in our experience it is worth continuing to practise at all ages. Drawing, painting and colouring are described as favourite activities by many teenagers and we know of many accomplished artists in different countries who show technical talent and considerable artistic expression. Hand-writing often continues to improve into adult life.

Developing recreational skills

Enjoying active sports and dance will bring many benefits for health and social contact in addition to the pleasure, self-confidence and the pride that may be gained from the activity. Success at sporting activities often seems linked with family interests and the opportunity to start early and engage in high levels of practice. We know many individuals who are exceptionally good skiers or swimmers, for example, and in each case their family gave them the opportunity to start early. Karen Gaffney, a young woman with exceptional swimming ability and stamina, has swum in an English Channel relay and her achievements can be found on her website (http://www.karengaffneyfoundation.com/). Sarah Duffen in the UK, now in her thirties, is competent in a range of sporting activities including swimming,

See also:

- An overview of the development of infants with Down syndrome (0-5 years) [DSii-01-02]
- An overview of the development of children with Down syndrome (5-11 years) [DSii-01-04]
- An overview of the development of teenagers with Down syndrome (11-16 years) [DSii-01-06]

Karen Gaffney, in centre

Sarah Duffen, 4th from right

water skiing, skiing and caving. She also drives a car and it may be that the range of physical activities that her parents encouraged from infancy provided her with the motor coordination and the visual-spatial skills to enable her to become a competent driver. Sarah also enjoys dancing, as does David de Graaf, in Holland. David is an accomplished cyclist and he is a musician. Harry Smale, in Jersey, now twelve years old, is an accomplished swimmer, skier, skateboarder and gymnast. He has been riding a bicycle since he was nine years old.

Dancing is an activity that is enjoyed by almost all the individuals with Down syndrome that we know and has the potential for enjoyment at whatever level of skill a person has achieved. Almost everyone enjoys a disco, while some achieve considerable skill in ballet and many display great talent in emotional expression through dance, mime and other performing arts.

David de Graaf

Harry Smale

Start early

It may be important to start activities such as swimming, dancing and gymnastics early. Many communities have opportunities for preschoolers to begin these activities. All the ordinary park games will also help, for example running, playing football, climbing and using swings/slides.

Teach by modelling

The advice to teach by demonstration is equally important for sporting and recreational activities. We have observed this in school physical education lessons and in dancing classes. Children with Down syndrome do not seem to find it easy to listen to or follow the teacher's verbal instruction – rather, they watch the other children and copy them. In a dancing class, the teacher often does demonstrate the steps but in school physical education lessons, much of the instruction is verbal and this may be much less effective.

Join clubs

Many communities have clubs for sport and recreation, and some teenagers and adults will enjoy ordinary community facilities with non-disabled peers, but some will prefer to join clubs for others with intellectual disability or the Special Olympics so that they have a chance to shine at the sport and to find close friendships.

Follow individual interests

With more children with Down syndrome being educated in mainstream school, they will have the chance to join in a wider range of activities than may be available in many special schools. This will provide greater chances to find out what they enjoy and where their talents lie.

It is never too late

One of the authors has an adult daughter with Down syndrome, Roberta, who walked very late (4 years) and had a 'poor gait', 'flat feet' and 'poor' posture throughout her childhood. We are not a sporty family and she led a rather sedentary life until she joined the Special Olympics team at the age of 21 and started training for running events. She then walked with a straight back rather than a slouch, lost her 'flat feet' and improved the 'normality' of her gait. (She also lost weight!) Roberta also became quite a good runner and won some medals in Special Olympic events. She was very proud of these achievements. This suggests two points – it is never too late

http://www.down-syndrome.info/library/dsii/12/01/

**DOWN SYNDROME
issues and
information**

to improve the way basic skills are performed, and the best way to improve is through ordinary activity and exercise. It is also never too late to think of encouraging adults to become more active. Readers might also like to note that Roberta considerably improved her fine motor skills as an adult. She was unable to copy her name legibly at 16 years of age but by her late twenties she could write very well, using small legible writing. Similarly, she could not tie shoelaces at 16 but now ties them as quickly and efficiently as a typically developing individual.

Developing employment skills

Built on basic skills

Many employment skills will be built on the everyday basic skills that individuals have acquired in order to make snacks and help in the kitchen, to work in school on the computer or to help with tasks such as cleaning, ironing and gardening. Many young people, especially those who may be making slower progress with cognitive and academic skills, enjoy being involved in the real-life daily tasks in the household. The message is essentially the same as for recreational skills – the earlier we encourage children to join in a range of daily activities and give them the opportunity to practise the better.

Learning in the workplace

The first job that Roberta had was as a care assistant in a care home for elderly people. Here she undertook simple cleaning tasks, cleaning wash basins and dusting, washing up and ironing as well as taking drinks to the elderly ladies in the house. In this job, she was using skills she had learned at home and in her independent living situation. In her next job, she needed to learn some new skills as she was now working in a shop selling children's clothes. She did some ironing and some pricing of clothes in this job and she developed her understanding of money in order to use the shop till. When she started her current job she had to learn more new skills as she was working with some machines that she had no previous experience of, she had to use her counting skills learned in adult education classes, and she built on her basic fine motor skills as she learned to put letters and leaflets together and to stuff envelopes. She was supported by a job coach for a few weeks until she was confident.

Do not underestimate abilities

The Down Syndrome Educational Trust recently began to employ adults with Down syndrome in its print workshop. This book has been assembled and packed by adults with Down syndrome. The six workers currently employed vary quite widely in ability and one young man often works with a partner as he does not have the fine motor skills for all the tasks – for example for picking up a single sheet of paper. However, his fellow workers are happy to work with him on tasks he cannot complete alone. All the workers learned all the tasks including operating several different machines much more quickly, and reached faster levels of work, than had been anticipated.

Conclusions

While motor development progresses more slowly for children with Down syndrome, the evidence that we have reviewed identifies a pattern of delay rather than specific difficulties, and many teenagers and adults eventually reach the same levels of skills as typically developing individuals, if they are given enough opportunities to practise. Research into the motor development of individuals with Down syndrome is limited, but some principles that can be used to guide effective intervention are emerging.

For everyone, movements develop and improve through active practice. It seems that individuals with Down syndrome often need more practice than typically developing individuals in order to consolidate their learning and achieve skilled movement patterns during childhood, therefore we need to create as many opportunities as possible to encourage active movement from infancy through to adult life. One research group stresses that it is possible that many adults with Down syndrome are performing at a lower level than is necessary, as they have shown dramatic improvements with practice in their studies.[5]

More information and ideas for encouraging basic motor skills and those that will enhance recreational and employment opportunities can be found in the age specific practical books on motor skills in the DSii series.

> **See also:**
> - *Motor skills development for infants with Down syndrome (0-5 years)* [DSii-12-02]
> - *Motor skills development for children with Down syndrome (5-11 years)* [DSii-12-03]
> - *Motor skills development for teenagers with Down syndrome (11-16 years)* [DSii-12-04]

Resources

The following books are available from the Down Syndrome Educational Trust:

Buckley, S. & Sacks, B. (2001). *An overview of the development of infants with Down syndrome (0-5 years)*. ISBN: 1-903806-02-X. The Down Syndrome Educational Trust: Portsmouth, UK.

Buckley, S. & Sacks, B. (2001). *An overview of the development of children with Down syndrome (5-11 years)*. ISBN: 1-903806-03-8. The Down Syndrome Educational Trust: Portsmouth, UK.

Buckley, S. & Sacks, B. (2002). *An overview of the development of teenagers with Down syndrome (11-16 years)*. ISBN: 1-903806-04-6. The Down Syndrome Educational Trust: Portsmouth, UK.

Medlen, J.E.G. (2002). *The Down syndrome nutrition handbook - a guide to promoting healthy lifestyles*. ISBN: 1-89062-723-2. Bethesda, MA: Woodbine House.

Bruni, M. (1998). *Fine motor skills in children with Down syndrome: A guide for parents and professionals*. ISBN: 1-890627-03-8. Bethesda, MA: Woodbine House.

Winders P. (1997). *Gross motor skills in children with Down syndrome: A guide for parents and professionals*. ISBN: 0-933149-81-6. Bethesda, MA: Woodbine House.

Newman, S. (1999). *Small steps forward*. ISBN: 1-85302-643-3. London: Jessica Kingsley.

Schwartz, S. & Miller, J.H. (1996). *The new language of toys - teaching communication skills to special needs children*. ISBN: 0-933149-73-5. Bethesda, MA: Woodbine House.

**DOWN SYNDROME
issues and
information**

References

1. Todorov, E. & Jordan, M.I. (2002). Optimal feedback control as a theory of motor co-ordination. *Nature Neuroscience*, 5(11), 1226-1235.

2. Graziano, M.S.A., Taylor, C.S.R. & Moore, T. (2002). Complex movements evoked by microstimulation of precentral cortex. *Neuron*, 34, 841-851.

3. Jordan, M.I. & Wolpert, D.M. (2000). Computational motor control. In M. S. Gazzaniga (Ed.) *The New Cognitive Neurosciences*. 2nd Edition. (pp. 601-618). Champaign, IL: Massachusetts Institute of Technology.

4. Ghez, C., Krakauer, J.W., Sainburg, R.L. & Ghilardi, M. (2000). Spatial representations and internal models of limb dynamics in motor learning. In M. S. Gazzaniga (Ed.) *The New Cognitive Neurosciences*. 2nd Edition. (pp. 501-514). Champaign, IL: Massachusetts Institute of Technology.

5. Latash, M.L. (2000). Motor coordination in Down syndrome: the role of adaptive changes. In D.J. Weeks, R. Chua & D. Elliott (Eds.) *Perceptual-motor behaviour in Down syndrome*. (pp. 199-224). Champaign, IL: Human Kinetics.

6. Dulaney, C.L. & Tomporowski, P.D. (2000). Attention and cognitive-skill acquisition. In D.J. Weeks, R. Chua & D. Elliott (Eds.) *Perceptual-motor behaviour in Down syndrome*. (pp. 175-198). Champaign, IL: Human Kinetics.

7. Campos, J.J., Anderson, D.I., Barbu-Roth, M.A., Hubbard, E.M., Hertenstein, M.J. and Witherington, D. (2000). Travel broadens the mind. *Infancy*, 1(2), 149-219.

8. Shumway-Cook, A. & Woollacott, M. H. (1985). Dynamics of postural control in child with Down syndrome. *Physical Therapy*, 65(9), 1315-1322.

9. Butterworth, G. & Cicchetti, D. (1978). Visual calibration of posture in normal and motor retarded Down syndrome infants. *Perception*, 7, 513-525.

10. Block, M.E. (1991). Motor development in children with Down syndrome: a review of the literature. *Adapted Physical Quarterly*, 8, 179-209.

11. Reid, G. & Block, M.E. (1996). Motor development and physical education. In B. Stratford & P. Gunn (Eds.) *New approaches to Down syndrome*. (pp. 309-340). London: Cassell.

12. Weeks, D.J., Chua, R. & Elliott, D. (2000). (Eds.) *Perceptual-motor behaviour in Down syndrome*. Champaign, IL: Human Kinetics.

13. Mauerberg-de Castro, E. & Angulo-Kinzler, R.M. (2000). Locomotor patterns of individuals with Down syndrome: effects of environmental and task constraints. In D.J. Weeks, R. Chua & D. Elliott (Eds.) *Perceptual-motor behaviour in Down syndrome*. (pp 71-98). Champaign, IL: Human Kinetics.

14. Welsh, T.N. & Elliott, D. (2000). Preparation and control of goal-directed limb movements in persons with Down syndrome. In D.J. Weeks, R. Chua & D. Elliott (Eds.) *Perceptual-motor behaviour in Down syndrome*. (pp. 49-70). Champaign, IL: Human Kinetics.

15. Almeida, G.L., Marconi, N.F., Tortoza, C. Ferreira, M.S., Gottlieb, G.L. & Corcos, D.M. (2000). Sensorimotor deficits in Down syndrome: implications for facilitating motor performance. In D.J. Weeks, R. Chua & D. Elliott (Eds.) *Perceptual-motor behaviour in Down syndrome*. (pp. 151-174). Champaign, IL: Human Kinetics.

16. Charlton, J.L., Ihsen, E. & Lavelle, B.M. (2000). Control of manual skills in children with Down syndrome. In D.J. Weeks, R. Chua & D. Elliott (Eds.) *Perceptual-motor behaviour in Down syndrome*. (pp. 25-48). Champaign, IL: Human Kinetics.

17. Anson, J.G. & Mawston, G.A. (2000). Patterns of muscle activation in simple reaction-time tasks. In D.J. Weeks, R. Chua & D. Elliott (Eds.) *Perceptual-motor behaviour in Down syndrome*. (pp. 3-24). Champaign, IL: Human Kinetics.

18. Cunningham, C. & Sloper, P. (1978). *Helping your handicapped baby*. London: Souvenir Press.

19. Berry, P., Andrews, R.J. & Gunn, V.P. (1980). *The early development of Down's syndrome in infants*. Final Report to National Health and Medical Research Council. St Lucia, Qld: University of Queensland, Fred and Eleanor Schonell Educational Research Centre.

20. Winders, P.C. (1997). *Gross motor skills in children with Down syndrome*. Bethesda, MA: Woodbine House.

21. Dyer, S., Gunn, P., Rauh, H. & Berry, P. (1990). Motor development in Down syndrome children: an analysis of the motor scale of the Bayley Scales of Infant Development. In A. Vermeer (Ed.) *Motor development, adapted physical activity and mental retardation: Vol. 30. Medicine and Sport Science.* (pp. 7-20). Basel, Switzerland: Karger.

22. Palisano, R.J., Walter, S.D., Russell, D.J., Rosenbaum, P.L., Gemus, M., Galuppi, B.E. & Cunningham, L. (2001). Gross motor function of children with Down syndrome: creation of motor growth curves. *Archives of Physical Medicine and Rehabilitation*, 82, 494-500.

23. Jobling, A. & Mon-Williams, M. (2000) Motor development in Down syndrome: a longitudinal perspective. In D.J. Weeks, R. Chua & D. Elliott (Eds.) *Perceptual-motor behaviour in Down syndrome*. (pp. 225-248). Champaign, IL: Human Kinetics.

24. Jobling, A. (1999). Attainment of motor proficiency in school aged children with Down syndrome. *Adapted Physical Quarterly*, 16, 344-361.

http://www.down-syndrome.info/library/dsii/12/01/

DSii-12-01-(en-gb)

29

25. Croce, R.V., Pitetti, K.H., Horvat, M. & Miller, J. (1996). Peak torque, average power, and hamstring/quadriceps ratios in non-disabled adults and adults with mental retardation. *Archives of Physical Medicine and Rehabilitation,* 77(4), 369-72.

26. Angelopolou, N., Tsimaras, V., Christoulas, K., Kokaridas, D. & Mandroukas, K. (1999). Isokinetic knee muscle strength of individuals with mental retardation, a comparative study. *Perceptual Motor Skills,* 88(3), 849-55.

27. Heath, M., Elliott, D., Weeks, D.J. & Chua, R. (2000). A functional systems approach to movement pathology in persons with Down syndrome. In D.J. Weeks, R. Chua & D. Elliott (Eds.) *Perceptual-motor behaviour in Down syndrome.* (pp. 305-320). Champaign, IL: Human Kinetics.

28. Peran, S., Gil, J.L., Ruiz, F. & Fernandez-Pastor, V. (1997). Development of physical response after athletics training in adolescents with Down syndrome. *Scandinavian Journal of Medicine and Science in Sports,* 7, 283-288.

29. Kerr, R. & Blais, C. (1985). Motor skill acquisition by individuals with Down syndrome. *American Journal of Mental Deficiency,* 90(3), 313-318.

30. Kerr, R. & Blais, C. (1987). Down syndrome and extended practice of a complex motor task. *American Journal of Mental Deficiency,* 91(6), 591-597.

31. Blais, C. & Kerr. R. (1986). Probability information in a complex motor task with respect to Down syndrome. *Journal of Human Movement Studies,* 12, 183-194.

32. Rauh, H., Rudinger, G., Bowman, T.G., Berry, P., Gunn, P.V. & Hayes, A. (1991). The development of Down's syndrome children. In M. Lamb & H. Keller (Eds.) *Infant development: perspectives from German speaking countries.* (pp. 329-355). Hillsdale, NJ: Lawrence Erlbaum Associates.

33. Connolly, B.H., Morgan, S. & Russell, F.F. (1984). Evaluation of children with Down syndrome who participated in an early intervention programme: second follow up study. *Physical Therapy,* 64(10), 1515-1519.

34. Wishart, J.G. (1993). Learning the hard way: avoidance strategies in young children with Down syndrome. *Down Syndrome Research and Practice,* 1(2), 47-55.

35. Henderson, S.E. (1985). Motor skill development. In D. Lane & B. Stratford (Eds.) *Current approaches to Down syndrome.* (pp. 187-218). London: Cassell.

36. Mon-Williams, M., Jobling, A. & Wann, J.P. (2000). Opthalmic factors in Down syndrome: a motoric perspective. In D.J. Weeks, R. Chua & D. Elliott (Eds.) *Perceptual-motor behaviour in Down syndrome.* (pp. 99-122). Champaign, IL: Human Kinetics.

37. Harris, S.R. (1981). Effects of neurodevelopmental therapy on motor performance of infants with Down's syndrome. *Developmental Medicine and Child Neurology,* 23, 477-483.

38. Ulrich, D.A., Ulrich, B.D., Angulo-Kinzler, R.M. & Yun, J. (2001). Treadmill training of infants with Down syndrome: evidence-based developmental outcomes. *Paediatrics,* 108 (5). Available online: http://www.pediatrics.org/cgi/content/full/108/5/e84.

39. Winders, P.C. (2001). The goal and opportunity of physical therapy for children with Down syndrome. *Down Syndrome Quarterly,* 6(2), 1-4.

40. Savelsburgh, G., van der Kamp, J., Ledebt. A. & Planinsek, T. (2000). Information-movement coupling in children with Down syndrome. In D.J. Weeks, R. Chua & D. Elliott (Eds.) *Perceptual-motor behaviour in Down syndrome.* (pp. 251-275). Champaign, IL: Human Kinetics.

41. Wade, M. G., Van Emmerik, R. & Kernozek, T. W. (2000). Atypical dynamics of motor behaviour in Down syndrome. In D.J. Weeks, R. Chua & D. Elliott (Eds.) *Perceptual-motor behaviour in Down syndrome.* (pp. 277-303). Champaign, IL: Human Kinetics.

42. Dyer, S.M. (1994). Physiological effects of a 13 week physical fitness programme on Down syndrome subjects. *Pediatric Exercise Science,* 6, 88-100.

43. Latash, M.L., Kang, N. & Patterson, D. (2002). Finger coordination in persons with Down syndrome: Atypical patterns of coordination and the effects of practice. *Experimental Brain Research,* 146, 345-355.

44. Buckley, S., Bird, G., Sacks, B. & Archer, T. (2002). The achievements of teenagers with Down syndrome: Part 2. *Down Syndrome News and Update,* 2(3), 90-96.

45. Maeda, F., Mazziotta, J. & Iacoboni, M. (2002). Transcranial magnetic stimulation studies of the human mirror neuron system. *International Congress Series,* 1232, 889-894.

DOWN SYNDROME issues and information